CLASSIC
StoryTellers

JACQUELINE WOODSON

Mitchell Lane
PUBLISHERS

P.O. Box 196
Hockessin, Delaware 19707

Titles in the Series

Beverly Cleary

E. B. White

Edgar Allan Poe

Ernest Hemingway

F. Scott Fitzgerald

Harriet Beecher Stowe

Jack London

Jacqueline Woodson

John Steinbeck

Judy Blume

Katherine Paterson

Mark Twain

Matt Christopher

Mildred Taylor

Nathaniel Hawthorne

Ray Bradbury

Stephen Crane

C L A S S I C
StoryTellers

JACQUELINE WOODSON

KaaVonia Hinton

Copyright © 2008 by Mitchell Lane Publishers, Inc. All rights reserved. No part of this book may be reproduced without written permission from the publisher. Printed and bound in the United States of America.

Printing   1   2   3   4   5   6   7   8   9

Library of Congress Cataloging-in-Publication Data
Hinton, KaaVonia.
    Jacqueline Woodson / by KaaVonia Hinton.
        p. cm. — (Classic storytellers)
    Includes bibliographical references and index.
    ISBN 978-1-58415-533-1 (library bound)
    1. Woodson, Jacqueline—Juvenile literature. 2. Authors, American—20th century—Biography—Juvenile literature. 3. African American women authors—Biography—Juvenile literature. I. Title.
PS3573.O64524Z68 2007
813'.54—dc22
[B]   2007000669

**KaaVonia Hinton (left) and
Jacqueline Woodson**

ABOUT THE AUTHOR: KaaVonia Hinton is an assistant professor in the Educational Curriculum and Instruction department at Old Dominion University in Norfolk, Virginia. She is the author of *Angela Johnson: Poetic Prose*.

AUTHOR'S NOTE: The author would like to thank Ms. Jacqueline Woodson for graciously sharing information about her life and work during interviews, e-mails, and telephone conversations.

PHOTO CREDITS: Cover, pp. 1, 3, 4, 6, 9—KaaVonia Hinton; pp. 12, 15, 20, 24, 26, 28, 36, 40—Courtesy of Jacqueline Woodson; p. 23—Hilary Silo.

Contents

JACQUELINE WOODSON

KaaVonia Hinton

Chapter 1   Dream Variations 7
            *FYInfo: Spike Lee 11
Chapter 2   Let America Be
            America Again 13
            FYInfo: The United
            States Presidency 19
Chapter 3   A Dream Deferred 21
            FYInfo: Dyslexia 27
Chapter 4   That's the Blues 29
            FYInfo: Langston Hughes 35
Chapter 5   Hold Fast to Dreams 37
            FYInfo: The Coretta Scott
            King Award 41
Chronology 42
Selected Works 42
Timeline in History 43
Chapter Notes 43
Further Reading 46
            For Young Adults 46
            Works Consulted 46
            On the Internet 47
Glossary 47
Index 48
*For Your Information

StoryTellers StoryTellers StoryTellers StoryTellers StoryTellers StoryTellers StoryTellers StoryTellers

Born in the midst of the modern civil rights movement, Jacqueline Woodson grew up aware of the inequalities that existed in the United States. She has used writing to express frustrations and concerns about issues important to her.

Chapter 1

DREAM VARIATIONS

Jacqueline Woodson was excited. Two producers were interested in using one of her books as the basis for a television program. Who would star in the miniseries? Where would it be filmed? Would Jacqueline be an integral part of the filming? A swarm of questions buzzed around in Jacqueline's mind. After writing the pilot episode, which producers used to generate funding for the project, her excitement waned until she completely forgot about the miniseries. Producers stopped calling. Thoughts about what the television program would be like diminished. "Then a lot of time passed," Jacqueline told *Scholastic Scope*. "I just saw an ad for *Miracle's Boys* and it blew me away."[1] The ad she saw was designed to promote the television show.

Several years earlier, in 2000, Woodson had published *Miracle's Boys,* a book about three half Latino/half African-American brothers: Ty'ree, Charlie, and Lafayette Bailey. Twenty-year-old Ty'ree puts his dream of attending MIT, the Massachusetts Institute of Technology, on hold to take care of his two brothers, sixteen-year-old Charlie and fourteen-year-old Lafayette. Their father died when the protagonist, Lafayette, was a baby. Their mother, Milagro (Spanish for *miracle*), got sick and died while Charlie was in a juvenile detention center. Woodson says she heard Lafayette's voice first when she began to write *Miracle's Boys*. It took her a while before she realized that Charlie had gone to a juvenile detention center after committing armed robbery and was in severe pain over his mother's death.[2] On her official Web site, Woodson says she wrote *Miracle's Boys* because she wanted to write a book about young men, poverty, pain, and loss. Equally important, she wanted "to write about three brothers who are funny, handsome, searching, and caring of one another."[3]

When asked about her depiction of the relationship between the brothers, Woodson responded, "Mostly I tried to create boys who were real. I used a bit from my own childhood and I guess I drew on the love I feel for my two brothers—one who is older and one who is younger. My older brother is kind of like Ty'ree and my younger one is a bit like both Charlie and Lafayette. I think there is a lot of me in Charlie too."[4]

In 2001, *Miracle's Boys* won the Coretta Scott King Award. This award is given to African-American authors and illustrators who have created excellent literature about black culture. In her acceptance speech, Woodson called the award a miracle: "Like Black people, it has survived and flourished. . . ."[5]

For Jacqueline Woodson, seeing the characters she created in the pages of her book appear on the television screen was a delightful experience, an experience she described as "surreal."[6] On her official Web site, she recalls, "I ended up spending far too much time on the set instead of being at home writing, but I got to sit in one of those fancy Director's chairs. (It didn't have my name on the back, though.) Some days, I took my family with me. The making of *Miracle's Boys* was definitely a high point in my summer."[7] While on the set, she met with Spike Lee, the director of the first and sixth episodes of the series, and the actors Pooch Hall (Ty'ree), Sean Nelson (Charlie), and Julito McCullum (Lafayette) to talk about how she conceived the characters in the novel. The actors told *Scholastic Scope* that reading Jacqueline

Actors from Miracle's Boys, *from left to right: Julito McCullum (Lafayette), Sean Nelson (Charlie), and Pooch Hall (Ty'ree)*

Woodson's novel helped them portray the characters convincingly.[8] "The story's so rich and so good that I felt proud just being a part of the project," Sean Nelson said.[9]

Directed by Neema Barnette, Bill Duke, Ernest Dickerson, Spike Lee, and LeVar Burton, and filmed on location in Harlem, the show premiered on February 18, 2005, on The N, a network for teens. In an interview on the DVD version of the series, Spike Lee said the series' executive producer, his wife, Tonya Lewis Lee, suggested that he read Woodson's book. After reading it, Lee praised Woodson's depiction of a multicultural community within the novel and expressed interest in being a part of the project.[10]

When the series begins, Ty'ree and Lafayette have planned a party to welcome Charlie home from the Mott Haven Juvenile Correctional Facility. Charlie's hostility and rude behavior toward family and friends earn him the name "Newcharlie." As the miniseries continues, Ty'ree, Lafayette, and Charlie struggle to repair the damage done to their family due to grief, hardship, and crime.

The series was a success. Guest appearances included Tiki Barber of the New York Giants and Jorge Posada of the New York Yankees. Rapper Nas wrote and performed the series' theme song. Critics praised the series for "eloquently captur[ing] the vibrant, tight-knit community of Harlem" and for handling mature themes "devoid of forced sentiment or blatant morality lessons."[11] Woodson said the series maintained the integrity of the novel, and that much of the scenery was similar to what she had imagined.[12]

When Jacqueline Woodson began to write, she never had the television screen in mind. She just wanted to write books about characters who were considered outside the mainstream. "For me it's about starting a dialogue so that people aren't feeling isolated and full of shame or completely alone. It's also about writing the kinds of books I would have liked to have read as a young person."[13]

FYInfo

Spike Lee

Jacqueline Woodson and Spike Lee talked frequently during the creation of the *Miracle's Boys* miniseries. Though Spike Lee was born Shelton Jackson Lee on March 20, 1957, in Atlanta, Georgia, he and Jacqueline both grew up in Brooklyn, New York. After living in Atlanta and Chicago briefly, Spike's parents moved to New York. A number of his popular films, such as *Do the Right Thing* and *Crooklyn,* are set in Brooklyn communities. Following in his grandfather's and father's footsteps, Spike enrolled in Morehouse College, the predominantly black college for men in Atlanta that Dr. Martin Luther King Jr. attended. Already interested in filmmaking, Spike attended the New York University film school after graduating from Morehouse. Though Spike did well in film school, initially he had trouble finding an agency that would support one of his projects.

Spike has written screenplays, nonfiction about the movies he has made, and children's picture books, but he is best known for directing and producing movies, commercials, documentaries, and music videos. His first film, *She's Gotta Have It,* was released in 1986 and earned eight million dollars. The box-office hit *School Daze* followed two years later. He has acted in most of his movies and included some of his family members

Spike Lee

in the casts, most frequently his sister, Joie Lee. Many of today's famous African-American actors—Halle Berry, Samuel L. Jackson, Denzel Washington, and Wesley Snipes—have acted in one or more of Spike's movies. *Mo' Better Blues* was the first film made by Spike's own production company, Forty Acres and a Mule. Many of his films focus on prejudice, racism, and other controversial social issues. Spike's success as a filmmaker has helped make it possible for a growing number of contemporary African-American filmmakers, such as John Singleton and Forest Whitaker, to work in the film industry today.

Jacqueline Woodson (center) and her third-grade class at PS 106 in Brooklyn, New York. That year, Ms. Moskowitz, her teacher, read The Little Match Girl *and* The Selfish Giant *to the class. Both books helped encourage Jacqueline's love of literacy.*

Chapter 2

LET AMERICA
BE AMERICA AGAIN

For civil rights history, 1963 was a pivotal year. In the midst of the modern civil rights movement, the United States of America was changing, but was it ready for change? Ready or not, the beginning of that year brought about the Twenty-fourth Amendment to the U.S. Constitution, an amendment that eliminated the poll tax put in place by several southern states after Reconstruction to hinder blacks from voting. The country was on its way toward ensuring that all of its citizens enjoyed the same rights.[1]

No one could foresee the frightening yet victorious months that lay ahead. Who could predict that Dr. Martin Luther King Jr. would be jailed after a peaceful protest and write one of the most persuasive letters ever written, "Letter from Birmingham Jail," in support of civil disobedience? Or that southern universities such as the University of Alabama would be desegregated?

Despite these accomplishments, people grew weary but determined when those not in support of change grew violent. No one was prepared for the deaths of civil rights leader Medgar Evers; of Addie Mae Collins,

Chapter 2   LET AMERICA BE AMERICA AGAIN

Denise McNair, Carole Robertson, and Cynthia Wesley, those four young girls killed while attending church in Birmingham, Alabama; or the countless others who are unknown.

On August 27, 1963, W.E.B. Du Bois, the man who is credited with chronicling African-American history and culture, died in Ghana. The day after Dubois's death, nearly 200,000 people participated in the March on Washington for Jobs and Freedom, where people from all around the world heard Dr. King's often-quoted speech, "I Have a Dream."[2]

The women's rights movement also sparked change in 1963 with the publication of Betty Friedan's *The Feminine Mystique,* a book that critiques images of American women portrayed in society. Friedan's book influenced the lives of individual women and society in general.[3]

Amidst all this societal change, Jacqueline Amanda Woodson was born on February 12, 1963. She was born into a time when people were yelling at the top of their lungs what Lena in Woodson's book *I Hadn't Meant to Tell You This* tells Marie: "We're all just people here."[4]

Jacqueline was born in Columbus, Ohio, to Jack and Mary Ann Woodson, but the couple's relationship ended a few months after her birth. Jacqueline was fifteen years old when she finally met her father. The breakup took Jacqueline and her two older siblings, Hope and Odella, to Greenville, South Carolina, to live with their grandparents. Shortly after the family relocated, Jacqueline's mother moved on to the Bushwick section of Brooklyn, New York, without her children; but by the time Jacqueline turned six, the family was reunited in New York and included a new member, Jacqueline's baby brother, Roman.[5]

Jacqueline visited her grandparents in South Carolina each summer until her grandfather died and her grandmother moved to New York during the 1970s. Jacqueline's mother worked long hours at Con Edison, so Jacqueline often spent time with her grandmother. In her acceptance speech for the 2001 Coretta Scott King Award,

"I wish...

they had
Alaga syrup
at school
too"

Alaga Syrup is rich in wholesome, energy-giving dextrose . . . that is so good for the children like Jacqueline Woodson pictured above. The sweet natural juices of field-ripened sugar cane give Alaga that smooth sweet taste no waffles, pancakes and biscuits. Write for our free recipe folder "Breakfast in a Jiffy." You will love the new ideas for getting Alaga Syrup in a variety of breakfast dishes.

ALAGA SYRUP COMPANY, P.O. Box 761, Montgomery, Alabama 36101

When she was two years old, Jacqueline was featured in a series of advertisements for Alaga Syrup in Ebony magazine.

Jacqueline said that when her grandmother moved to New York, "She brought with her . . . a garden variety of ideas that would plant themselves firmly in my brothers and sister and me. For me, what grew was a belief that I could be a writer of short stories and poems—and maybe even one day whole books!"[6]

Jacqueline and her grandparents were close. Her picture book *Sweet, Sweet Memory* is loosely based on feelings she had when her grandfather died. Jacqueline's grandparents were Jehovah's Witnesses, so she was encouraged to attend Bible study and other meetings offered at the Kingdom Hall three times a week throughout her youth. In an autobiographical statement for the *Eighth Book of Junior Authors and Illustrators,* Jacqueline said her religion prevented her from celebrating birthdays and holidays, pledging allegiance to the flag, and participating in war. She wrote, "I was about eleven or twelve and I was standing up on a swing, pumping my knees hard so that the swing went high into the air and I was singing 'America the Beautiful' at the top of my lungs. I loved that song! And I loved 'The Star-Spangled Banner.' Maybe I loved them so much because I wasn't allowed to sing either of these songs."[7]

Jacqueline once said, "When I was young, my grandmother's first question in the morning was, 'Did you say your prayers this morning?' If my lie didn't come quick enough, she sent me back to bed, where, with the biggest pout on that side of Brooklyn, I reluctantly thanked the forces for giving me another day."[8]

Jacqueline's experiences as a Jehovah's Witness have influenced her writing. In her novel *Hush,* the protagonist, Toswiah, and her family have a difficult time when they are forced to exchange their old way of life in Denver for a new one in another city. To cope with change, Toswiah's mother finds strength in being a Jehovah's Witness.

Similarly, Jacqueline's short story "On Earth" focuses on Carlene and her brothers and sister, young people who are nurtured by a grandmother who insists that they attend Kingdom Hall regularly. Separated from their mother, being Jehovah's Witnesses helps connect the children to their grandmother and their new home in South Carolina. Jacqueline says "On Earth" is not autobiographical, but "there is an element of autobiography to it. My years as a Witness were complicated ones. Years I neither regret nor miss. Being a Witness is a part of my young adult world that remains with me—tender and complex as adolescence itself."[9]

Jacqueline's love of seeing words on paper became clear at three years old when her sister taught her to write her own name. "I just loved the power of that . . . of being able to put a letter on the page and that letter meaning something. It was the physical act of writing for me that happened first. Not so much telling stories but actually having the tools with which to create a landscape of words."[10] During her childhood, she enjoyed writing so much, "I wrote on everything and everywhere. I remember my uncle catching me writing my name in graffiti on the side of a building. (It was not pretty for me when my mother found out.) I wrote on paper bags and my shoes and denim binders. I chalked stories across sidewalks and penciled tiny tales in notebook margins. I loved and still love watching words flower into sentences and sentences blossom into stories."[11]

Jacqueline said in a speech given at a children's literature conference in Georgia that she loved attending elementary school at Public School 106. She also enjoyed playing games like freeze tag, kick the can, double dutch, softball, and basketball with her friends. Her love of writing and her active imagination became noticeable to others during this time. On her Web site she says she wrote a poem about Dr. Martin Luther King Jr., but no one believed she wrote it, not even her teacher. She eventually received a prize for writing the poem, and she suddenly understood that writing could be rewarding. She says the experience gave her confidence, and it still does: "Sometimes, when I'm sitting at my desk for long hours and nothing's coming to me, I remember my fifth grade teacher, the way her eyes lit up when she said 'This is really good.' The way, I—the skinny girl in the back of the classroom who was always getting into trouble for talking or missed homework assignments—sat up a little straighter, folded my hands on the desk, smiled and began to believe in me."[12] Jacqueline was such a good writer, she was appointed editor of her class's literary magazine.

Jacqueline loved to read just as much as she loved to write. The library in her neighborhood was like a second home to her. Though she enjoyed books by Judy Blume, Hans Christian Andersen, and Oscar Wilde, she craved books that included African-American characters. "The first time I read *Sounder*, I was in grade school and I remember thinking, 'But this is all wrong. How come his mother isn't hugging him?' The book, written by a white author, paints a heartbreaking picture of a black family in the south. There is no touching anywhere in it and even as a child, I knew this book was about no black family I'd ever met or ever wanted to meet."[13]

Two books that inspired Jacqueline to become a writer were Sounder, by William H. Armstrong, and Stevie, by John Steptoe.

She eventually found titles by Virginia Hamilton, James Baldwin, Mildred Taylor, Langston Hughes, and Rosa Guy, authors who changed her life. In her acceptance speech for the 2001 Coretta Scott King Award, she said she learned from these writers, "who didn't know they were giving a young black girl from Brooklyn the message that she, too, could do this."[14]

Her understanding of her invisibility in books and society grew, and she became angry. Gerald Ford was the country's new president. After President Richard Nixon resigned, Jacqueline had hoped that George McGovern would take his place. She was only nine or ten at the time, but she listened as everyone in her neighborhood agreed that McGovern wanted to help blacks. With President Ford in office, Jacqueline believed her community would never get the help it needed. Where was the justice in this? she wondered.

To Jacqueline, this experience suggested that the American dream would never be a reality for some people. In an essay, she wrote, "For the first time, I had believed that America was going to begin to exist as a nation, that we could live as Martin Luther King Jr. had dreamed—in solidarity, coexisting, helping each other."[15] When this didn't happen, Jacqueline became sad and withdrawn. "The word *democracy* no longer existed for me," she wrote.[16]

Jacqueline was also aware of the Vietnam War, and she watched family and friends return sad and broken. She turned to writing to help her make sense of the world. She spent most of her free time writing poetry and "anti-American songs."[17] She also began reading books, such as John Steptoe's *Stevie,* that included the experiences of marginal people, people of color and those who were poor. *Stevie* was particularly important to Jacqueline because it was among the first books she read that included African-American vernacular. "The book was a big inspiration. It was the first time I read a book that had the language of my people in it."[18] Like *Stevie,* many of Jacqueline's books give voice to Americans who use variations of the English language.

FYInfo

The United States Presidency

Commander in chief, chief executive, and *head of state* are all names for the president of the United States. Running the country is a difficult job, and there are requirements that must be met before someone can run for president. The requirements, which also apply to the vice president, are found in the U.S. Constitution. A candidate must be at least thirty-five years old, a natural-born citizen, and a United States resident for at least fourteen years. The president serves for four years and can be reelected only once. Voters vote for the president in November of an election year. If there is a tie, the House of Representatives selects the president. The president and vice president are sworn into office in an inaugural ceremony held on January 20. The president lives and works in the White House, which is located on Pennsylvania Avenue in Washington, D.C., while the vice president lives in the vice-presidential mansion on Massachusetts Avenue, also in Washington, D.C. Both the president and the vice president earn salaries determined by the U.S. Congress.

Sometimes the vice president has to serve as president because the president has died, resigned, or been impeached or removed from office. A vice president will also finish a president's term if the president has a problem that keeps him from serving as president. In 1972, when Jacqueline was in elementary school, George McGovern ran for president and lost to Richard Nixon. Two years later, in 1974, President Nixon resigned and the vice president, Gerald Ford, finished Nixon's term.

All of the first forty-three presidents were white males, but African Americans such as Jesse Jackson and Shirley Chisholm have run for president; so has a Japanese American, Patsy Mink. Women such as Geraldine Ferraro have also run for vice president. Hillary Rodham Clinton, senator and former first lady, would run for president in 2008 against African-American Barack Obama.

Shirley Chisholm

Jacqueline warms up before a softball game. She loves sports so much, she jokes, that if she were not a writer, she'd be an NBA player.

Chapter 3

A DREAM DEFERRED

During adolescence, Jacqueline found books like *The Bluest Eye* by Toni Morrison, *If Beale Street Could Talk* by James Baldwin, and other influential works by African Americans. She eventually edited an anthology titled *A Way Out of No Way: Writings about Growing Up Black in America.* The book includes over fifteen stories, poems, and excerpts from novels by notable African-American authors such as Langston Hughes, Toni Cade Bambara, Ntozake Shange, and Ernest J. Gaines. In an interview on the Penguin Group Web site, Jacqueline said, "My young adult years had the biggest impact on me of any period in my life and I remember so much about them."[1]

In the introduction to *A Way Out of No Way: Writings about Growing Up Black in America,* Jacqueline describes herself reading quietly alone in a room in her home while her family engaged in different, often noisy, activities.[2] Though she was an avid reader, during childhood she was a struggling reader. "I read slowly. Sometimes I still do. I might have had dyslexia, but while growing up during the seventies, I wasn't tested."[3]

Chapter 3   A DREAM DEFERRED

When Jacqueline had trouble understanding her homework, her older sister helped her. Jacqueline once told an audience at a literature conference that she "was somewhat of a teacher's nightmare. I was the one who talked too much, who snuck food from my desk thinking the teacher wouldn't hear the crinkle of the wrapper. I was the child who didn't have the patience to think through a sum and found it more gratifying to guess."[4]

In high school, Jacqueline loved sports, but her mother would not allow her to run track because she had a heart murmur. Jacqueline still managed to be active in extracurricular activities. She was a cheerleader, and she dated the captain of the basketball team. "Growing up I always felt there's a way in which you belong—I definitely had my clique of girls, and I was a cheerleader and dated a basketball player—but it always felt like I was outside watching that and never quite belonging," she said in a *Publishers Weekly* article.[5]

While Jacqueline attended high school, she met an influential teacher named Kirk Miller. He encouraged Jacqueline to choose a career that would allow her to do work she enjoyed doing. "That moment it hit me that [writing] was the thing I loved doing more than anything."[6]

After Jacqueline graduated from Bushwick High School, she attended Adelphi University in Garden City, New York, where she majored in English with a concentration in British Literature and Middle English. Adelphi was close to home, and the college offered Jacqueline an academic scholarship. During her freshman year, she also earned a track scholarship. She participated in several events, including running the quarter mile, the 200, the 800, the four-by-four relay, and the four-by-two relay, as well as cross country.[7] At one point, Jacqueline could run 400 meters in 58 seconds. She says, "Winning medals was . . . a plus."[8] Still athletic, Jacqueline began training in the martial art Poekoelan, a form of Indonesian street fighting, in 1993.[9] Her other pastimes include sewing and watching NBA and WNBA basketball.[10]

After receiving her acceptance letter from Adelphi, Jacqueline decided to become a teacher, hoping to teach seventh grade. Meanwhile she continued to write. While in college, Jacqueline met

Jacqueline has often attended the MacDowell Colony in New Hampshire, a place devoted to nurturing writers, musicians, and other artists.

women who were lesbians and realized that she was also a lesbian, a woman who is attracted to other women. Jacqueline met her partner, Juliet, when Juliet was a medical student. Now Juliet is a doctor of internal medicine, and she and Jacqueline are raising their daughter, Toshi Georgiana, in Brooklyn.[11]

Jacqueline's book *Show Way,* a 2006 Newbery Honor Book, is a tribute to several generations of women in her family. A Show Way is a quilt that was used to lead slaves to freedom. Jacqueline's great-grandmother, Soonie, learned to sew quilts, and the skill was passed down from generation to generation until it reached Jacqueline. The book ends with an illustration of Jacqueline and Toshi as Jacqueline passes the family story, and talents, on to her daughter.

Jacqueline graduated from Adelphi University in 1985 with a degree in English. When reflecting on her time at Adelphi, she told Lois Stover that she hadn't liked it there. She felt isolated because the college lacked a community of people of color, among the student body and the faculty, with whom Jacqueline could bond. However, pledging the sorority Alpha Kappa Alpha did help her form friendships with other black women at Adelphi.[12]

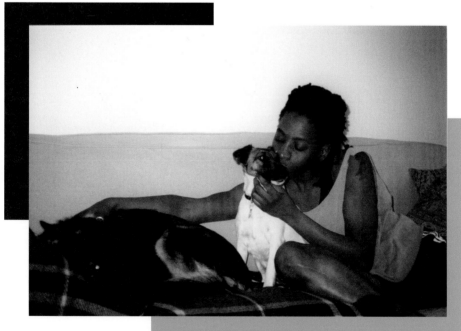

Jacqueline loves animals, including her dogs. Maus, who is lying down on the couch, died in 2006 at age thirteen.

After graduation, Jacqueline took a job at Kirchoff/Wohlberg, a children's literature packaging company. She continued to write while working there.[13] She wanted to learn more about writing for children, so she took a class at the New School of Social Research. One night the teacher, Bunny Gable, read some of Jacqueline's writing aloud to the class. An editor from a publishing company was there and asked to read the entire manuscript. The editor liked what she read and decided to publish it. The book was published as *Last Summer with Maizon* in 1990.[14]

Finding time to write while working several jobs was a challenge for Jacqueline. She often worked at least three jobs at one time, mostly word processing, so that she could have a few hours to devote to writing. She also worked with homeless and runaway youths while writing her second novel, *The Dear One,* about twelve-year-old Afeni and her growing friendship with Rebecca, a pregnant teen from Harlem. When *The Dear One* was published, there were few writers of young adult fiction that humanized teenage pregnancy or that depicted pregnant African-American teens as knowledgeable human beings with hope for their futures.

Jacqueline thought she would be able to stop working so many jobs after selling her first book, but she was not able to become a full-time writer until she had published eight books. She began writing *Maizon at Blue Hill* at a difficult point in her life. The novel is the second part of the Maizon trilogy and focuses on Maizon's separation from family and friends while attending boarding school. Like Maizon, Jacqueline was separated from most of her loved ones, having moved from New York to California. Once Jacqueline realized the isolation was impacting her writing, she returned home to Brooklyn.[15]

She eventually received several opportunities to attend the MacDowell Colony in New Hampshire and also spent time at the Fine Arts Work Center in Provincetown, Massachusetts, during the early 1990s. Both of these places, where writers and artists can work on their craft without distraction, offered her time to grow as a writer.[16]

Jacqueline autographs copies of Last Summer with Maizon *at her first book-signing in Brooklyn, New York.*

By 1994, Jacqueline had published several stories in *The Kenyon Review;* the novels in the Maizon trilogy—*Last Summer with Maizon, Maizon at Blue Hill,* and *Between Madison and Palmetto;* and *I Hadn't Meant to Tell You This.* She had also begun receiving awards and citations, such as the *Kenyon Review* Award, a Coretta Scott King Honor Book citation, and *Publishers Weekly* Best Books citations. Jacqueline's dream of becoming a successful writer was finally being realized.

FYInfo

Dyslexia

Dyslexia is a learning disability thought to be hereditary, or passed down from one's relatives. It affects people of all ages, races, ethnicities, and income levels. In 1896, a British doctor named William Pringle Morgan became the first to publish information about dyslexia, though he thought it was a condition resulting from poor vision. Modern researchers are still trying to learn more about the disability. Some scholars believe dyslexia occurs when a baby is growing inside its mother, while others claim it may be caused by the way a person's brain is formed.

Someone who is dyslexic learns differently. Though a person with dyslexia is usually of average to above-average intelligence, his or her brain does not process information the way that a non-dyslexic person's brain does.

People experience dyslexia in varying ways. A person with dyslexia may have difficulty reading, writing, speaking, listening, or learning math. Dyslexic people may also have trouble recalling the alphabet, sounds of letters, or months of the year. Reversing letters and numbers when writing, confusing directions such as right and left, writing illegibly, having trouble understanding time, and failing to recognize words are all signs that suggest a person might be dyslexic.

If it is suspected that a person has dyslexia, there are a number of tests professionals can administer. Although there is no cure for dyslexia, teaching strategies are available to help people with dyslexia learn to read and write effectively. Important teaching strategies include instruction in letter and sound recognition and reading comprehension.

Some people with dyslexia are exceptional artists, athletes, engineers, actors, and musicians. Artist and scholar Leonardo da Vinci, inventor Thomas Edison, and writer Hans Christian Andersen are now thought to have been dyslexic. Actor Danny Glover, comedian Whoopi Goldberg, actor Tom Cruise, and athlete Magic Johnson all have dyslexia.

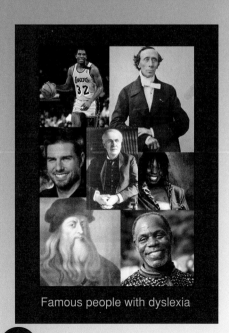

Famous people with dyslexia

Jacqueline on her porch in Provincetown, Massachusetts, in 1992. She worked on some of her books, including I Hadn't Meant to Tell You This *and* The House You Pass on the Way, *in Provincetown.*

Chapter 4

THAT'S THE BLUES

Most of Jacqueline's work is contemporary realistic fiction, books about how people live in our society today. She gets her ideas from conversations she has within her community, what she notices about the world, and things that are important to her. Jacqueline gets frustrated when critics say she writes about tough issues. "It's interesting to me when people say I write about 'tough' issues or that the issues are 'edgy' because, for me, they are things we talk about in my community every day."[1]

Her earlier novels feature adolescent girls. *Last Summer with Maizon* focuses on friendship, death, grief, and community. On her official Web site, Jacqueline says she wrote the Maizon trilogy because, "growing up, there were very few books about black girls and even fewer about people like the people I knew in my neighborhood in Brooklyn. I wanted to write about the people I loved and the neighborhood that had been my home for many years."[2] In an article published in *Obsidian III,* Jacqueline wrote, "I want to get under the skin of the young girl whose self-esteem is fast-fading before our society's fictions do. I want to show her herself and who she can be. I want to show her that the history of our society was not written to include her and her recognition of this is not herself going crazy but a truth."[3]

Novels such as *I Hadn't Meant to Tell You This,* its sequel, *Lena,* and *The House You Pass on the Way* depict girls who tackle racism, exploitation, homelessness, sexuality, pregnancy, and abuse. In *I Hadn't Meant to Tell You This,* Lena tells Marie, the protagonist, that her father is molesting her (touching her in inappropriate places). Jacqueline is passionate about this topic and believes it should be discussed in literature. "In our society three out of four girls experience some form of sexual abuse by the time they are adults. That's a high number of people, so the fact that it's not being talked about in literature makes people [unconscious of it]."[4]

The House You Pass on the Way is Jacqueline's only novel set in the South, despite her strong connection to the area. Fourteen-year-old Staggerlee seems different from others in Sweet Gum. She is biracial, her mother is one of only a few white women in town, and her famous grandparents died while fighting for civil rights. When her cousin Trout comes for a visit, Staggerlee begins to wonder about her sexuality, another part of her identity that might set her apart from others in the community.

Jacqueline says that most of her early novels "stayed close to her own life."[5] Curious about her ability to explore serious concerns from a male character's perspective, Jacqueline wrote *From the Notebooks of Melanin Sun.* "It meant doing some hard work—the work of being a writer—stepping into another's shoes and seeing the world through their eyes," she wrote in the *Eighth Book of Junior Authors and Illustrators*.[6] Critics praised her depiction of a sensitive young man trying to make sense of adolescence and his mother's relationship with a white woman. Jacqueline gave Melanin her love of recording her thoughts and feelings in journals: "I usually give my characters something that is important to me, like journaling," she explains.[7] She has kept a journal since childhood. "When I open my journal, it feels like I'm a child going into my room and closing the door. Exaltation. Exhale. Freedom inside my space. It's a place where I can tell the truth, 100 percent, and be who I am," she continues.[8]

If You Come Softly, a love story featuring an African-American male and a white Jewish girl, followed. Jacqueline describes the book as a retelling of William Shakespeare's *Romeo and Juliet.*[9] As in *Romeo and Juliet,* tragedy and death separate fifteen-year-old Jeremiah and Ellie when Jeremiah is killed by a police officer. *Behind You,* a sequel to *If You Come Softly,* was published in 2004. In this novel, Jeremiah watches as his family and friends try to move on after his death.

An article in the *New York Times Magazine* gave Jacqueline the idea for *Hush,* her second novel that includes racist and violent police officers.[10] When the protagonist's father testifies against his co-workers, who he claims shot an innocent black male, the family is admitted into the Witness Protection Program. The program drastically changes their lives.

Many of Jacqueline's picture books also suggest injustices within society. *Visiting Day,* about a girl whose dad is in prison, was written to combat some of the shame children with relatives in prison often feel. When Jacqueline was a child, she wasn't allowed to tell anyone outside her family that her uncle was in prison. "The issue of the high number of black men in prison is a big issue, and not only because the numbers are so imbalanced in terms of how many people of color are incarcerated, but also because in families, it doesn't get talked about. So there is a lot of shame around that, and I think the issue of shame is a big issue for me because I don't think anyone should feel it for any reason."[11]

Jacqueline never set out to write for a particular audience. "I write for everybody, but it seems I am most prolific in the young adult category. Even my work for adults has the voice of a young adult character. It just seems like that's where I found my voice as a writer."[12]

She sent the stories she wrote for adults to magazines and journals. Several were first published in the *Kenyon Review* and served as the basis for her book for adults, *Autobiography of a Family Photo.* Her stories published for adolescents are included in several anthologies: *Am I Blue? Coming Out from the Silence,* edited by Marion Dane Bauer; *Girls Got Game: Sports Stories & Poems,* edited by Sue Macy; and *The Color of Absence: 12 Stories about Loss and Hope,* edited by James Howe.

She usually writes several books at one time. The books she works on simultaneously are usually of different genres, such as novels or picture books, and for different audiences. "I never work on one thing at a time because I get bored," she says.[13] She has written essays, articles, short stories, novels, and picture books. Writing poetry is the hardest for her, though she writes poetry in her journals and has used some of it to create the postcards Marie's mother sends her in *I Hadn't Meant to Tell You This.*

In an interview in *BookPage,* Jacqueline said, "I hated poetry growing up . . . I think I was afraid of it . . . I didn't understand it."[14] Langston Hughes's poetry was the first verse she understood and enjoyed. She says she recited his poem "I, Too" during a school assembly when she was in third grade.[15] But her meager interest in poetry did not stop her from writing *Locomotion,* a book written entirely in different types of poetry: free verse, sonnets, and haiku. The protagonist, Lonnie Collins Motion, uses poetry to make sense of his life after the tragic death of his parents.

Poetry is now a part of Jacqueline's writing process. "When I'm writing picture books, I read a lot of poetry because poetry is very direct and very spare. I also try to get myself into the rhythm of the book. *The Other Side* (2000) begins with 'That summer the fence that stretched through our town seemed bigger.' That first image suggests that readers ask, 'What fence?' 'What town?' 'What's going on?' 'Why did it seem bigger?' So all of a sudden, as a reader you start asking all of these questions, which pull you into the book. Poetry does the same thing."[16] During a live chat with teens at the New York Public Library, Jacqueline said she wrote *The Other Side* about her experiences in Brooklyn. "The story was written thinking about the way segregation exists in the present day. But once I saw [E. B.] Lewis' beautiful illustrations, I didn't want to change them, so it became a story about

Between 1990 and 2005, Jacqueline had twenty-five books published. Many of them had been translated into other languages, including Italian, Spanish, Dutch, Tagalog, Mandarin, and Turkish.

the past,"[17] about segregation and Jim Crow laws. In *The Other Side,* two young girls, one black and one white, befriend each other despite their mothers' warnings against crossing racial barriers.

Jacqueline believes young readers know when they are ready to think critically about the subjects in her books. "People say you can't put all that material into a book for young people because it'll distress them or they won't be able to absorb it all. But I believe children's minds compartmentalize—they will put stuff away until they're ready to deal with it."[18]

Though Jacqueline writes about topics that many authors are criticized for including in their books, reviewers often praise Jacqueline's depiction of social ills, emphasizing her portrayal of "sympathetic characters [who] make the big questions more accessible for teens to examine."[19] Yet, Jacqueline says she does feel her work is censored. She has spoken at schools that do not put her books in the school library, and she noticed a decrease in requests to visit schools after certain books, such as *I Hadn't Meant to Tell You This* and *From the Notebooks of Melanin Sun,* were published.[20] Because Jacqueline's books have been censored or challenged, her story "July Saturday," about a possible teen arsonist, was included in Judy Blume's 1999 book *Places I Never Meant to Be: Original Stories by Censored Writers.*

She also believes that earlier in her career self-censorship impacted her work. "At first I thought that if I was writing for young adults, then I would have to censor myself."[21] Self-censoring, or refusing to write about a topic because she believed it was too difficult or mature for youths to read about, stifled her creativity, preventing her from telling the types of stories she believes are important.

With each book, Jacqueline has grown as a writer. When *The Dear One* was republished in 2003, Jacqueline was critical of her early writing. "It was raggedy," she said. "I've grown as a writer. You never stop learning how to do this better. It's about pushing against walls and challenging yourself and also challenging the world."[22] One of her challenges included enrolling in a screenwriting class.

FYInfo

Langston Hughes

Langston Hughes is one of Jacqueline Woodson's favorite poets. He lived in New York, just as Jacqueline does. He moved there in 1921 to attend Columbia University. Later, he became one of the most prolific writers of the Harlem Renaissance, an artistic movement in Harlem, New York, during the 1920s. Born James Langston Hughes in Joplin, Missouri, on February 1, 1902, he spent much of his youth in Lawrence, Kansas, with his grandmother. Hughes graduated from Central High School in Cleveland, Ohio, where he published poems in the school magazine. By the time he was a young adult, he was already on his way to becoming a nationally published poet, with poems appearing in the National Association for the Advancement of Colored People (NAACP) magazine *The Crisis,* edited by W.E.B. Du Bois, and the children's magazine *The Brownies' Book.* Among his first publications was "The Negro Speaks of Rivers," written during a trip to visit his father in Mexico. He traveled to different parts of the world, including South America, Africa, and France, before he attended Lincoln University, a historically black college in Pennsylvania. He graduated in 1929.

Langston wrote in every genre imaginable: plays, short stories, novels, autobiographies, essays, criticism, and, of course, poems. His use of blues and jazz musical forms, African-American vernacular, and topics and issues of importance to African Americans are seen in poems such as "The Weary Blues," "Let America Be America Again," "Madam and the Phone Bill," and "Mother to Son." *The Dream Keeper and Other Poems,* which was first published in 1932, is one of his poetry books written especially for young people.

Before Langston's death in New York on May 22, 1967, he had mentored several generations of writers, from Gwendolyn Brooks to Alice Walker and James Emanuel. He won many awards throughout his career, including the Harmon Gold Medal for Literature in 1931 and the Spingarn Medal, awarded by the NAACP, in 1960.

Gwendolyn Brooks
and Langston Hughes

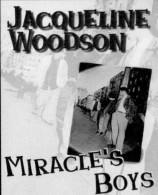

Jacqueline has received several Coretta Scott King Honor citations, but in 2001 she and illustrator Bryan Collier both received Coretta Scott King Awards. While she was honored for Miracle's Boys, Collier received an award for the illustrations in Uptown. The awards ceremony was actually canceled that year because there was a strike at the hotel in which it was to be held. Coretta Scott King, the committee, Jacqueline, and Bryan refused to cross the picket line.

Chapter 5

HOLD FAST TO DREAMS

Jacqueline knew at an early age that she wanted to be a writer. By 1994, when her sixth book for young people, *I Hadn't Meant to Tell You This,* was published and had been named a Coretta Scott King Honor Book, it was clear she had achieved her goal. Her next novel, *From the Notebooks of Melanin Sun,* was both a Coretta Scott King Honor Book and a Jane Addams Children's Book Award Honor Book. In 1996, she was listed in *Granta* magazine as one of its Fifty Best American Authors. Jacqueline has also edited several books, including *Just a Writer's Thing: A Collection of Prose and Poetry from the National Book Foundation's 1995 Summer Writing Camp,* which she coedited with writer Norma Fox Mazer.

In 2001, after winning two honor citations from the Coretta Scott King Committee, she received the Coretta Scott King Award for *Miracle's Boys,* which also won the *Los Angeles Times* Book Prize. A year later, *Hush* was a National Book Award finalist. Jacqueline also had books named to many prestigious lists: the American Library Association's Best Books for Young Adults,

Publishers Weekly's Best Books of the Year, and the CBC/NCSS
(Children's Book Council and National Council for the Social Studies)
Notable Children's Trade Books in the Field of Social Studies.
Jacqueline's picture book *Coming on Home Soon* was named a Caldecott
Honor Book in 2005, and *Show Way* was named a Newbery Honor
Book in 2006.

   With over twenty-five books to her credit, Jacqueline achieved
arguably her highest honor in 2006 when she received the Margaret A.
Edwards Award. This award, sponsored by *School Library Journal* and
named after a celebrated librarian, was established in 1988 and honors
lifetime achievement in writing for young adults. Jacqueline was
honored and awarded $2,000 at the American Library Association's
annual conference. According to the official Web site of the American
Library Association, Jacqueline received this honor because her "books
are powerful, groundbreaking and very personal explorations of the
many ways in which identity and friendship transcend the limits of
stereotype. . . . Her captivating and richly drawn characters struggle
and grow and celebrate who they are in the world, and reveal to readers
exciting possibilities for their own lives."[1]

   Jacqueline appreciates being honored, but she admits that
winning awards and receiving recognition comes with a price. In a
speech given at the University of Georgia in Athens, Jacqueline
wondered, "How do you get back to who you were before the
recognition?" At a point in her career when activities "get in the way of
the actual writing," she simply longs for more time to write.[2]

   Although the demands on her time are great, Jacqueline enjoys
visiting schools and talking to young people about books. She hopes
her novels make readers think and question assumptions about social
issues and life in general.[3]

   Though Jacqueline began working as an editorial assistant and a
freelance writer after college, she did eventually become a teacher. She
has taught writing to students of all ages at the National Book
Foundation's summer writing camp, Goddard College, Vermont
College at Norwich University, and Eugene Lang College.[4] She often

Coming on Home Soon *earned a Caldecott Honor Medal, the highest honor given for illustrations in a picture book.*

Jacqueline's picture book, Show Way, *earned the Newbery Honor Medal, given to outstanding books for young people.*

guides her students through an analysis of excerpts from various literary works by authors such as Carson McCullers, Jamaica Kincaid, and Raymond Carver. Jacqueline encourages her students to be aware of their own emotional response to literature, just as she, as a beginning reader, was struck by *The Little Match Girl*. Once they realize their personal response, Jacqueline encourages students to examine the literature to determine how the author evoked such an emotion. What words and events did the author include that caused the emotional reaction readers feel? she asks.[5]

An Na, award-winning author of *A Step from Heaven*, credits Jacqueline for teaching her the craft of writing spare and poetic prose.

Jacqueline travels all around the country talking to young people about her books and encouraging them to become lifelong readers and writers.

In an interview published in the paperback edition of her book, Na said, "I had a really amazing writer, Jacqueline Woodson, as my first writing teacher. She kicked my butt. She was the one who taught me to pare down my language, look at the metaphors, and see how a vignette packs a multilayered punch."[6]

Writers have also mentored Jacqueline. She felt that some, such as James Baldwin, mentored from the pages of their books. These writers seemed to speak to Jacqueline, urging her to believe that she could become an author, too. Other authors, such as Virginia Hamilton and her husband, Arnold Adoff, were physically present when they mentored Jacqueline. Hamilton endorsed *From the Notebooks of Melanin Sun* when she made positive comments about it and allowed the publishing company to print them on the book's cover. Jacqueline says Hamilton and Adoff were "there from book one" with advice and encouragement.[7]

Jacqueline's dream has come true. She once said, "I want to leave a sign of having been here. The rest of my life is committed to changing the way the world thinks, one reader at a time."[8] Her status as an award-winning author of books translated into a number of languages is evidence that she is doing just that.

FYInfo

The Coretta Scott King Award

Established in 1969 by African-American children's librarians Glyndon Greer and Mabel McKissick, the Coretta Scott King Award honors civil rights leader Dr. Martin Luther King Jr. and his wife, Mrs. Coretta Scott King. The purpose of the award is to "affirm new talent and to offer visibility to excellence in writing and/or illustration which otherwise might be formally unacknowledged within a given year."[9]

Since 1970, the award has been presented each year to a worthy African-American author, and since 1974, to an African-American illustrator of exceptional books. The award did not become official and recognized by the American Library Association until 1982. Authors and illustrators are selected by the Coretta Scott King Committee of the Ethnic Multicultural Information Exchange Round Table of the American Library Association. The award, which includes a plaque and $1,000, is presented at the American Library Association's annual conference each June.

Jacqueline has had three books named Coretta Scott King Honor Books, and she won the Coretta Scott King Award for *Miracle's Boys* in 2001. The awards ceremony that year was scheduled for June 19 at a Marriott hotel in San Francisco, California. Hotel employees were engaged at that time in a dispute with the Marriott corporation, and a number of librarians spoke of

Coretta Scott King

boycotting the ceremony. It was finally canceled when Mrs. King refused to attend, explaining, "I have long supported the struggles of working people for union representation, decent wages and working conditions, and the thought of recipients of the Awards having to cross a picket line of working people to receive their honors is very disturbing to me."[10]

Mrs. King was born on April 27, 1927, in Perry County, Alabama. She studied music at Antioch College and Boston's New England Conservatory of Music. After her husband's death, she continued much of the work he had started, including leading a march in Memphis, Tennessee, just days after his assassination, and speaking out against social injustices. She died in Mexico on January 30, 2006. She was seventy-eight years old.

CHRONOLOGY

1963	Born on February 12 in Columbus, Ohio; moves to Greenville, South Carolina, shortly after birth
1968	Moves with mother to Brooklyn, New York
1973	Maternal grandmother moves to Brooklyn
1985	Graduates from Adelphi University
1990	Publishes *Last Summer with Maizon* and *Martin Luther King, Jr., and His Birthday*
1991	Publishes *The Dear One*
1992	Publishes *Maizon at Blue Hill*
1994	Publishes *The Book Chase* and *I Hadn't Meant to Tell You This*
1995	*I Hadn't Meant to Tell You This* is named a Coretta Scott King Honor Book; publishes *From the Notebooks of Melanin Sun*
1996	Publishes *A Way Out of No Way: Writings about Growing Up Black in America*; *From the Notebooks of Melanin Sun* is named a Coretta Scott King Honor Book and a Jane Addams Children's Book Award Honor Book
1997	Publishes *The House You Pass on the Way*, which wins the Lambda Literary Award
1998	Publishes *If You Come Softly*
2000	Publishes *Miracle's Boys*
2001	*Miracle's Boys* wins the Coretta Scott King Award and the Los Angeles Times Book Prize
2002	Daughter Toshi is born; publishes *Hush*, which is named a National Book Award finalist
2003	Publishes *Locomotion*, which is named a National Book Award finalist and a Coretta Scott King Honor Book
2004	Publishes *Behind You*
2005	Publishes *Show Way*, which is named a Newbery Honor Book
2006	Receives Margaret A. Edwards Award for lifetime contribution to young adult literature
2007	Is expecting a second child; and is working on several books, including *The Potential for Light* and *After Tupac and D Foster*

SELECTED WORKS

1990	*Last Summer with Maizon*	**1997**	*The House You Pass on the Way*
1991	*The Dear One*	**1998**	*If You Come Softly*
1992	*Maizon at Blue Hill*	**2000**	*Miracle's Boys*
1993	*Between Madison and Palmetto*	**2003**	*Locomotion*
1994	*I Hadn't Meant to Tell You This*	**2004**	*Behind You*
1995	*From the Notebooks of Melanin Sun*	**2005**	*Show Way*

TIMELINE IN HISTORY

1896 Supreme Court supports the decision of *Plessy v. Ferguson,* which states that separate but equal facilities for blacks and whites are legal; Alpha Kappa Alpha sorority for African-American women is established at Howard University.

1918 The first elected president of South Africa, Nelson Mandela, is born.

1920 Women in the United States obtain the right to vote.

1929 Civil rights leader Dr. Martin Luther King Jr. is born.

1930 The Harlem Renaissance ends.

1954 The Supreme Court's *Brown v. Board of Education* decision requires the desegregation of schools in the United States.

1955 Bus boycott begins in Montgomery, Alabama.

1957 Vietnam War begins.

1960 Four black students at North Carolina Agricultural & Technical State University try to order food at a Woolworth lunch counter that only serves whites.

1964 Civil Rights Act is passed.

1973 Vietnam War ends.

1978 Karol Józef Wojtyla is named John Paul II and serves as Pope until his death in 2005.

1993 Toni Morrison wins the Nobel Prize in Literature.

1996 The first mammal is cloned from DNA.

2001 The World Trade Center in New York is destroyed when hijacked airplanes crash into it; actress Halle Berry becomes the first African-American woman to win the Academy Award for Best Actress.

2005 Hurricane Katrina ravages New Orleans, Louisiana, and other parts of the Gulf Coast.

2006 Condoleezza Rice, the first African-American woman to serve as secretary of state, encourages Israel, Hezbollah, and Lebanon to arrange an agreement to stop fighting.

2007 The nation celebrates the 50th anniversary of the desegregation of Central High School in Little Rock, Arkansas.

CHAPTER NOTES

Chapter 1 Dream Variations

1. Lisa Feder-Feitel, "5 Questions for the Author," *Scholastic Scope*, February 7, 2005, p. 17.

2. Ibid.

3. Jacqueline Woodson, *Young Adult Titles,* http://jacquelinewoodson.com/ya.shtml

4. Penguin Group (USA), "An Interview with Jacqueline Woodson," http://us.penguingroup.com/static/rguides/us/jacqueline_woodson.html#interview

5. Jacqueline Woodson, "Miracles: Coretta Scott King Award Acceptance Speech," *School Library Journal,* August 1, 2001, p. 58.

6. Personal communication with the author, April 3, 2006.

7. Jacqueline Woodson, *Special Projects,* http://jacquelinewoodson.com/specproj.shtml

8. Feder-Feitel, p. 17.

CHAPTER NOTES

9. Marie Morreale, "Meet the Brothers of *Miracle's Boys,*" http:// teacher.scholastic.com/scholasticnews/ indepth/miraclesboys.asp

10. *Miracle's Boys,* DVD (Hollywood, California: Paramount Pictures, 2005).

11. Laura Fries, "Review of *Miracle's Boys,*" *Daily Variety,* February 18, 2005, p. 6.

12. *Miracle's Boys,* DVD (Hollywood, California: Paramount Pictures, 2005).

13. KaaVonia Hinton, "Jacqueline Woodson: Keeping It Real about Social Issues," *Journal of Children's Literature,* vol. 30, 2004, p. 27.

Chapter 2 Let America Be America Again

1. Jeffrey C. Stewart, *1001 Things Everyone Should Know About African American History* (New York: Doubleday, 1996), p. 124.

2. Ibid., p. 153.

3. Betty Friedan, *The Feminine Mystique* (New York: W. W. Norton, 1963).

4. Jacqueline Woodson, *I Hadn't Meant to Tell You This* (New York: Delacorte, 1994), p. 59.

5. Lois Thomas Stover, *Jacqueline Woodson: "The Real Thing"* (Lanham, Maryland: Scarecrow Press, 2003), p. 2.

6. Jacqueline Woodson, "Miracles: Coretta Scott King Award Acceptance Speech," *School Library Journal,* August 1, 2001, p. 58.

7. Connie Rockman, ed., *Eighth Book of Junior Authors and Illustrators* (Bronx, New York: H. W. Wilson Company, 2000), p. 560.

8. Jacqueline Woodson, "Miracles: Coretta Scott King Award Acceptance Speech," *School Library Journal,* August 1, 2001, p. 57.

9. Marilyn Singer, ed., *I Believe in Water: Twelve Brushes with Religion* (New York: HarperCollins, 2000), p. 275.

10. Jennifer M. Brown, "Jacqueline Woodson: From Outsider to Insider," *Publishers Weekly,* vol. 249, February 11, 2002, p. 156.

11. Jacqueline Woodson, *My Biography,* http://jacquelinewoodson.com/bio.shtml

12. Ibid.

13. Jacqueline Woodson, "Fictions," *Obsidian III: Literature in the African Diaspora,* vol. 3, Spring/Summer 2001, p. 49.

14. Jacqueline Woodson, "Miracles: Coretta Scott King Award Acceptance Speech," *School Library Journal,* August 1, 2001, p. 58.

15. Jacqueline Woodson, "A Sign of Having Been Here," *Horn Book Magazine,* vol. 71, November/December 1995, p. 711.

16. Ibid.

17. Ibid.

18. Jacqueline Woodson, unpublished speech, April 21, 2006, University of Georgia, Athens, Georgia.

Chapter 3 A Dream Deferred

1. Penguin Group (USA), "An Interview with Jacqueline Woodson," http:// us.penguingroup.com/static/rguides/us/ jacqueline_woodson.html#interview

2. Jacqueline Woodson, ed., *A Way Out of No Way: Writings about Growing Up Black in America* (New York: Henry Holt, 1996), p. 4.

3. Personal communication with the author, April 22, 2006.

4. Jacqueline Woodson, unpublished speech, April 21, 2006, University of Georgia, Athens, Georgia.

5. Jennifer M. Brown, "Jacqueline Woodson: From Outsider to Insider," *Publishers Weekly,* vol. 249, February 11, 2002, p. 156.

6. Ibid.

7. Sue Macy, ed., *Girls Got Game: Sports Stories & Poems* (New York: Henry Holt, 2001), p. 90.

8. Ibid.

9. Lois Thomas Stover, *Jacqueline Woodson: "The Real Thing"* (Lanham, Maryland: Scarecrow Press, 2003), p. 8.

10. Macy, p. 90.

11. Jacqueline Woodson, "Motherhood, My Way: After Years of Longing a Lesbian Sister Fulfills Her Wish to Start a Family of Her Own," *Essence,* vol. 34, December 2003, p. 182.

12. Jacqueline Woodson, "Common Ground," *Essence,* vol. 30, May 1999, p. 212.

CHAPTER NOTES

13. Stover, p. 9.

14. Stover, pp. 9–10.

15. Paula W. Graham, ed., *Speaking of Journals: Children's Book Writers Talk about Their Diaries, Notebooks, and Sketchbooks* (Honesdale, Pennsylvania: Boyds Mills Press, 1999), p. 64.

16. Stover, p. 11.

Chapter 4 That's the Blues

1. KaaVonia Hinton, "Jacqueline Woodson: Keeping It Real about Social Issues," *Journal of Children's Literature,* vol. 30, 2004, p. 27.

2. Jacqueline Woodson, *Middle Grade Titles,* http://jacquelinewoodson.com/mg.shtml

3. Jacqueline Woodson, "Fictions," *Obsidian III: Literature in the African Diaspora,* vol. 3, Spring/Summer 2001, p. 49.

4. Hinton, p. 27.

5. Connie Rockman, ed., *Eighth Book of Junior Authors and Illustrators* (Bronx, New York: H. W. Wilson Company, 2000), p. 560.

6. Ibid.

7. Paula W. Graham, ed., *Speaking of Journals: Children's Book Writers Talk about Their Diaries, Notebooks, and Sketchbooks* (Honesdale, Pennsylvania: Boyds Mills Press, 1999), p. 65.

8. Ibid., pp. 63–64.

9. Penguin Group (USA), "An Interview with Jacqueline Woodson," http://us.penguingroup.com/static/rguides/us/jacqueline_woodson.html#interview

10. Ibid.

11. Hinton, p. 27.

12. Ibid.

13. Ibid.

14. Heidi Henneman, "Poetry in Motion," http://www.bookpage.com/0302bp/jacqueline_woodson.html

15. Jacqueline Woodson, ed., *A Way Out of No Way: Writings about Growing Up Black in America* (New York: Henry Holt, 1996), p. 168.

16. Hinton, p. 27.

17. New York Public Library, "Transcript from NYPL's Author Chat with Jacqueline Woodson Held July 23rd, 2003," http://summerreading.nypl.org/read2003/chats/woodson.cfm

18. Diane R. Paylor, "Bold Type: Jacqueline Woodson's 'Girl Stories,' " *Ms. Magazine,* vol. 5, November/December 1994, p. 77.

19. Jennifer M. Brown, "Jacqueline Woodson: From Outsider to Insider," *Publishers Weekly,* vol. 249, February 11, 2002, p. 157.

20. Jacqueline Woodson, "A Sign of Having Been Here," *Horn Book Magazine,* vol. 71, November/December 1995, p. 713.

21. Samiya A. Bashir, "Tough Issues, Tender Minds," *Black Issues Book Review,* vol. 3, May/June 2001, p. 79.

22. Hinton, p. 29.

Chapter 5 Hold Fast to Dreams

1. American Library Association, *Margaret A. Edwards Award,* http://www.ala.org/yalsa/edwards

2. Jacqueline Woodson, unpublished speech, April 21, 2006, University of Georgia, Athens, Georgia.

3. KaaVonia Hinton, "Jacqueline Woodson: Keeping It Real about Social Issues," *Journal of Children's Literature,* vol. 30, 2004, p. 28.

4. Lois Thomas Stover, *Jacqueline Woodson: "The Real Thing"* (Lanham, Maryland: Scarecrow Press, 2003), pp. 14–15.

5. Personal communication with the author, April 21, 2006.

6. An Na, *A Step from Heaven* (New York: Penguin, 2002), p. 156.

7. Jacqueline Woodson, unpublished speech, April 21, 2006, University of Georgia, Athens, Georgia.

8. Jacqueline Woodson, "A Sign of Having Been Here," *Horn Book Magazine,* vol. 71, November/December 1995, p. 715.

9. American Library Association, *Coretta Scott King Award,* http://www.ala.org/ala/emiert/cskbookawards/cskawardhome.htm

10. Rick Margolis, "King Breakfast Cancelled," http://www.schoollibraryjournal.com/article/CA90689.html

FURTHER READING

For Young Adults

Blume, Judy, ed. *Places I Never Meant to Be: Original Stories by Censored Writers.* New York: Simon & Schuster, 1999.

Lee, Spike, and Kaleem Aftab. *Spike Lee: That's My Story and I'm Sticking to It.* New York: W. W. Norton, 2005.

Gibson, Karen. *Langston Hughes.* Hockessin, Delaware: Mitchell Lane Publishers, 2006.

Works Consulted

Personal interviews and e-mail correspondence with Jacqueline Woodson by the author, November 2003 and April 2006 through November 2007. In addition, the author used the following sources:

"A Partner in the Dream." *The Virginian-Pilot.* February 1, 2006.

Bashir, Samiya A. "Tough Issues, Tender Minds." *Black Issues Book Review.* Volume 3, May/June 2001.

Brown, Jennifer M. "Jacqueline Woodson: From Outsider to Insider." *Publishers Weekly.* Volume 249, February 11, 2002.

Feder-Feitel, Lisa. "5 Questions for the Author." *Scholastic Scope.* February 7, 2005.

Friedan, Betty. *The Feminine Mystique.* New York: W. W. Norton, 1963.

Fries, Laura. "Review of *Miracle's Boys.*" *Daily Variety.* February 18, 2005.

Graham, Paula W., ed. *Speaking of Journals: Children's Book Writers Talk about Their Diaries, Notebooks, and Sketchbooks.* Honesdale, Pennsylvania: Boyds Mills Press, 1999.

Hinton, KaaVonia. "Jacqueline Woodson: Keeping It Real about Social Issues." *Journal of Children's Literature.* Volume 30, 2004.

Landau, Elaine. *Dyslexia.* New York: Franklin Watts, 2004.

Macy, Sue, ed. *Girls Got Game: Sports Stories & Poems.* New York: Henry Holt, 2001.

Miracle's Boys. DVD. Hollywood, California: Paramount Pictures, 2005.

Na, An. *A Step from Heaven.* New York: Penguin, 2002.

Paylor, Diane R. "Bold Type: Jacqueline Woodson's 'Girl Stories.'" *Ms. Magazine.* Volume 5, November/December 1994.

Rockman, Connie, ed. *Eighth Book of Junior Authors and Illustrators.* Bronx, New York: H. W. Wilson Company, 2000.

Singer, Marilyn, ed. *I Believe in Water: Twelve Brushes with Religion.* New York: HarperCollins, 2000.

Stewart, Jeffrey C. *1001 Things Everyone Should Know About African American History.* New York: Doubleday, 1996.

Stover, Lois Thomas. *Jacqueline Woodson: "The Real Thing."* Lanham, Maryland: Scarecrow Press, 2003.

Strom, Sharon Hartman. *Women's Rights.* Westport, Connecticut: Greenwood Press, 2003.

Woodson, Jacqueline. "A Sign of Having Been Here." *Horn Book Magazine.* Volume 71, November/December 1995.

———, ed. *A Way Out of No Way: Writings about Growing Up Black in America.* New York: Henry Holt, 1996.

———. "Common Ground." *Essence.* Volume 30, May 1999.

———. "Fictions." *Obsidian III: Literature in the African Diaspora.* Volume 3, Spring/Summer 2001.

———. *I Hadn't Meant to Tell You This.* New York: Delacorte, 1994.

———. "Miracles: Coretta Scott King Award Acceptance Speech." *School Library Journal.* August 1, 2001.

———. "Motherhood, My Way: After Years of Longing a Lesbian Sister Fulfills Her Wish to Start a Family of Her Own." *Essence.* Volume 34, December 2003.

———. Unpublished speech. Athens, Georgia: University of Georgia, April 21, 2006.

On the Internet

American Library Association: *Coretta Scott King Award* http://www.ala.org/ala/emiert/corettascottkingbookawards/winnersa/newtalentawarda/newtalentaward.htm

American Library Association: *Margaret A. Edwards Award* http://www.ala.org/yalsa/edwards

Henneman, Heidi. "Poetry in Motion" http://www.bookpage.com/0302bp/jacqueline_woodson.html

Jacqueline Woodson http://jacquelinewoodson.com

Margolis, Rick. "King Breakfast Cancelled" http://www.schoollibraryjournal.com/article/CA90689.html

Morreale, Marie. "Meet the Brothers of *Miracle's Boys*" http://teacher.scholastic.com/scholasticnews/indepth/miraclesboys.asp

New York Public Library: "Transcript from NYPL's Author Chat with Jacqueline Woodson Held July 23rd, 2003" http://summerreading.nypl.org/read2003/chats/woodson.cfm

Penguin Group (USA): "An Interview with Jacqueline Woodson" http://us.penguingroup.com/static/rguides/us/jacqueline_woodson.html#interview

Scholastic: *Jacqueline Woodson Biography* http://content.scholastic.com/browse/contributor.jsp?id=3590

Taylor, Deborah. "Jacqueline Woodson" http://www.schoollibraryjournal.com/article/CA6338688.html

GLOSSARY

administer (aad-MIH-nih-stur)
To give; to offer.

blatant (BLAYT-ent)
Noticeable and offensive.

civil disobedience (SIH-vul dis-oh-BEE-dee-unts)
Nonviolent refusal to obey governmental laws.

controversial (kahn-truh-VUR-shuhl)
Something that causes disagreement because people have strong opinions about it.

desegregate (dee-SEH-grih-gayt)
To become open to members of different races and ethnic groups.

devoid (dih-VOYD)
Lacking; empty.

integrity (in-TEG-rih-tee)
The trait of being honest.

miniseries (MIH-nee-sihr-eez)
A number of episodes of a particular television program; a television program that tells a story in multiple episodes.

prolific (proh-LIH-fik)
Very productive.

sentiment (SEN-tih-ment)
Emotion; feeling.

solidarity (sah-lih-DAYR-ih-tee)
The loyalty and support that holds a group of people together.

vernacular (vur-NAA-kyoo-lur)
The everyday language spoken by a group of people.

vibrant (VY-brunt)
Lively; exciting.

wane (WAYN)
To decrease in size or amount.

INDEX

Adelphi University 22–24

Adoff, Arnold 40

Alpha Kappa Alpha 24

Baldwin, James 18, 21, 40

The Bluest Eye 21

Blume, Judy 17, 34

Brooklyn, New York 11–12,14–15, 17–18, 23, 25–26, 29, 32

Censorship 34

Civil Rights Movement 6, 13, 30, 41

Collier, Bryan 36

Columbus, Ohio 14

Coretta Scott King Award 8, 14, 18, 36, 37, 41

Dyslexia 21, 27

Friedan, Betty 14

Gable, Bunny 25

Greenville, South Carolina 14

Hamilton, Virginia 18, 40

Hughes, Langston 18, 21, 32, 35

If Beale Street Could Talk 21

Jane Addams Children's Book Award 37

Jehovah's Witness 15–16

Kenyon Review 26, 31

King, Coretta Scott 36, 41

King, Martin Luther, Jr. 11, 13, 16, 18, 41

Lee, Spike 8, 10, 11

Lewis, E. B. 32, 39

MacDowell Colony 23, 25

Margaret A. Edwards Award 38

Mazer, Norma Fox 37

Miniseries 7, 8, 9, 10, 11

Morrison, Toni 21

Na, An 39, 40

National Book Foundation 37–38

Presidency 19

Racism 11, 30

Woodson, Jacqueline
awards for 8, 26, 36, 37–38, 39, 40
birth of 14
childhood of 8, 12, 14–17, 20–21, 30

children of 23–24

college graduation 25

education of .. 12, 16–17, 19, 22–25, 32

first book 25–26, 29

grandparents of 14–15, 23

hobbies of 22

parents of 14

partner of 23

siblings of 14

sports of 20, 22

teaching of 38, 39, 40

works of
Autobiography of a Family Photo ... 31
Behind You 31
Between Madison and Palmetto 26
The Book Chase 42
Coming on Home Soon 38, 39
The Dear One 25, 34
From the Notebooks of Melanin Sun 30, 34, 37, 40
The House You Pass on the Way 28, 30
Hush 15, 31, 37
I Hadn't Meant to Tell You This 14, 26, 28, 30, 32, 34, 37
If You Come Softly 31
"July Saturday" 34
Just a Writer's Thing: A Collection of Prose and Poetry from the National Book Foundation's 1995 Summer Writing Camp 37
Last Summer with Maizon 25–26, 29
Lena 30
Locomotion 32
Maizon at Blue Hill 25–26
Miracle's Boys 7–8, 9, 11, 37, 41
The Other Side 32–33
Show Way 23–24, 38, 39
Visiting Day 31
A Way Out of No Way: Writings about Growing Up Black in America 21